Achieving a Sustainable Competitive Advantage

The Playbook for the CEO

by Robert K Bennett

Table of Contents

Introduction

When I was in the telecommunications industry, I watched as Western Union, an old and once very powerful company, entered the decline phase of its existence while demand for data communications services was at the same time going through the roof. I soon saw other companies suffer this same fate.

I looked into the situation further and discovered these statistics from the U.S. Census Bureau.

- There are 28 million businesses in the U S
    - 22 million are sole proprietor businesses with no employees
    - 6 million have fewer than 500 employees
    - Only 20,000 have more than 500 employees
- Small businesses have generated over 65% of the net new jobs since 1995
- More employer businesses shut down than start up each month (This is a significant contributor to the weakness in the job market.
- More than 500,000 new businesses are started each month
- More than 125,000 of these are employer firms
- 30% of employer firms fail within 2 years
- 50% of employer firms fail within 5 years
- 66% of employer firms fail within 10 years and
- 75% of employer firms fail within 15 years
- By 1983, 1/3 of companies on the 1970 Fortune 500 list were gone.
- Only 30% of family owned and operated businesses make it into the 3rd generation

George Santayana, a Spanish philosopher, said, "Those who do not remember the past are condemned to repeat it."

I'm not asking that you totally believe that your company will fade away and die. Although there is that possibility, it is asking too much to ask someone to believe that about their company. On the other hand, you don't want to repeat history just because you ignored it. You can hedge against the decline-and-die-out stages of the business life cycle. Keep reading to learn how.

I also discovered that not all companies suffer this fate and that the companies who remained at the top of their game adhered to most if not all seven principles. Most of these companies were still led by their founders. When the founder left the scene, those who succeeded the founder sometimes departed from some of those principles and when they did, performance declined. (Apple?)

Once I was able to recognize and delineate these seven principles, I asked this question. How can I help companies institutionalize these principles into their day-to-day business? How can I turn an art into a science? This led to the creation and development of Strategic Alignment, a business planning and management system that will help a company develop an innovative and unique business model focused on customer need. If faithfully followed, Strategic Alignment will lead to a sustainable competitive advantage and extend the life expectancy of the company.

Seven Guiding Principles

Do you remember TWA and Pan Am? Years ago, they were both large, international airlines. Today, they are, for all practical purposes, gone.

Digital Equipment Company (DEC) was once the dominant manufacturer of mini-computers. With DEC's products, the "glass palace" which contained (in the majority of cases) an IBM mainframe computer disappeared and each department could have its own mini-computer. As we now know, this phase evolved into our current phase where every desktop has its own computer. So, did DEC, a manufacturer of computers, lead the way into personal computers (PCs)? No. DEC is gone. (So are mini-computers).

Radio Corporation of America (RCA) was a very large manufacturer of consumer electronics. It is gone. Its name may remain, but the company is gone.

You may not remember the real Western Union. In the early 20th century, it was one of the largest and most powerful companies in the U.S. The Western Union you see now is not that company. Another company bought the rights to use the name. Western Union, the company, is gone.

AT&T, the American Telephone & Telegraph Company - Ma Bell - has been swallowed up into one of her children, SBC (Southwestern Bell, which then changed its name to AT&T).

What do all of these companies have in common?

They lost contact with their customers.

They failed to understand the shifting needs of their customers.

They failed to define the future for their customers.

Other companies, sometimes after redefining themselves, continue to perform at the top of their game.

By 1993, IBM's annual net loss reached a record $8 billion. Cost management and streamlining became a chief concern. And IBM considered splitting its divisions into separate independent businesses.

Louis V. Gerstner, Jr. arrived as IBM's chairman and CEO on April 1, 1993. Soon after he arrived, he had to take dramatic action to stabilize the company. These steps included rebuilding IBM's product line, continuing to shrink the workforce and making significant cost reductions. Despite mounting pressure to split IBM into separate, independent companies, Gerstner decided to keep the company together. Gerstner fundamentally redefined IBM's mission and business model and aligned the company to that mission. IBM began thriving once more.

Gerstner showed us that a company which has entered the decline phase and has begun the death spiral (which starts with gradual reductions in sales and revenue and then sees that reduction accelerate and finally cascade into bankruptcy) can be saved and the death spiral halted. However, the salvation requires a drastic and fundamental change in the company's mission, vision, and business model.

Steve Jobs was one of the founders of Apple Computer. In the early 1980's, at the urging of the Board of Directors (who thought the company needed "adult leadership"), Jobs brought John Sculley, a well-known management veteran, into Apple as CEO. As the Macintosh took off in sales and became a big hit, John Sculley felt Jobs was hurting the company and persuaded the board to strip him of all power. John Sculley tried to change the discipline of the company by controlling costs, reducing overhead, and rationalizing product lines. Jobs left Apple and started a new computer company called NeXT. He also bought Pixar for $10 million. Meanwhile, Sculley was dismissed, and the Apple Board hired Gil Amelio as Apple CEO with the mission to enhance shareholder value. (As we will discuss later, if your primary purpose and mission is to enhance shareholder value, you won't succeed). Predictably, Amelio failed. After Gil Amelio's departure, Apple purchased NeXT Computer, probably to bring Jobs back into Apple. Jobs returned to Apple as interim CEO. Subsequently, the word "interim" was removed from his title, and he re-energized the company.

In 1965, Yale University undergraduate Frederick W. Smith wrote a term paper about the passenger route systems used by most airfreight shippers, which he viewed as economically inadequate. Smith wrote of the need for shippers to have a system designed specifically for airfreight that could accommodate time-sensitive shipments such as medicines, computer parts and electronics.

Federal Express was incorporated in June of 1971 and officially began operations on April 17, 1973, with the launch of 14 small aircraft from Memphis International Airport. On that night, Federal Express delivered 186 packages to 25 U.S. cities from Rochester, NY, to Miami, FL. Although the company did not show a profit until July 1975, it soon became the premier carrier of high-priority goods in the marketplace and the standard setter for the industry it established. FedEx has a customer-focused mission. It remains a powerhouse in overnight delivery and is still led by CEO Fred Smith.

Why do some companies soar and others languish? Why do winners who have dominated their markets and industry for some time – companies such as Sears, Toys R Us, and perhaps McDonald's - suddenly stumble and begin a long period of decline which is apparently irreversible?

When he was IBM Chairman, Sam Palmisano called a sustainable competitive advantage "the holy grail of strategic thinking". He said that the central question for every CEO is, "how do you come up with a business model that differentiates you and that creates value for your customers, and, by doing that, puts you in a unique position in your industry?"

Consistently dominant winners have obviously achieved a sustainable competitive advantage. But how did they do it? And what is it about them that gives them their sustainable competitive advantage?

For years, I searched for the secret and finally uncovered Seven Guiding Principles, which are followed by most, if not all, companies who have consistently remained at the top of their industries. Furthermore, I have learned that if other companies adopt and adhere to these Seven Principles, they, too, are likely to experience sudden, dramatic, and sustainable improvement in their results and will overtake and pass other companies on their way to the top.

As a result, I developed Strategic Alignment, which if faithfully followed will result in the company following the Seven Principles. Strategic Alignment leads to a sustainable competitive advantage by producing a unique, customer centric business model that cannot be duplicated, because it incorporates the psyche of the company's leader. Furthermore, following Strategic Alignment keeps a company in the Growth stage of the Business Life Cycle and avoids entering into the Mature and Decline stages.

The Seven Guiding Principles of Top Performing Companies

1 - Successful companies keep their central focus and top priority on the customer and his/her need.

2 - Successful companies identify and select their customers.

3 - Successful companies differentiate how they serve the recognized need of the selected and identified customer in ways that provide real, recognizable value to the customer.

4 - Successful companies develop and promulgate prioritized values that truly reflect the business values of the leadership and tell the employees how the company will operate on a day-to-day basis.

5 - All of the decisions, initiatives, directions, investments, plans, procedures, policies, actions, and reactions of the company are brought into alignment with the central focus and the mission.

6 – The leadership preaches the mission throughout the company with a religious-like zeal and commitment. All employees buy into the mission. And the buy-in takes place from the top down – in that order.

7 - Every employee, including the CEO, subordinates his or her needs to the needs of the company.

Before we discuss the Seven Guiding Principles in more depth, there are a couple of cautionary notes.

This is not sloganeering. It is not sufficient to write the Principles down, frame them, and hang them on the wall in the reception area, down the hall, or in the employees' break room. Successful companies fervently believe in these Guiding Principles and follow them in everything they do, 100% of the time. To do less is, at best, a waste of time and, more often, actually harmful.

At first glance, following these Principles may seem simple and easy. Knowing what to do may be easy. Consistently doing it 100% of the time is not so easy.

Some people have maintained that these Principles and the underlying business theory are naïve and overly simplistic. I take the opposite view. I believe that too many business leaders and managers overcomplicate business to their detriment and the detriment of the business. As we will discuss at great length later, everyone in a business – *every employee* – must know, understand, accept, and ultimately embrace

who the company is,

what the company plans to become,

who the company's customer is,

what that customer needs, and

how the company will serve that need in ways that are different from the other competitors who attempt to serve those same customers..

In my model, these and other concepts are embodied in the Mission. In order to achieve as wide an understanding and acceptance as possible of the Mission, leadership and management should strive to simplify its Principles and underlying business theory as much as possible, reducing miscommunication, misunderstanding, and confusion to a minimum.

Let's review and discuss each Principle.

Successful companies keep their central focus and top priority on the customer and his/her need

Every company has three main constituencies – customers, employees, and owners. Sure, there are other constituencies, such as suppliers and the community within which the company resides and operates, but most agree that the primary constituencies are customers, employees and owners.

A fundamental key to becoming and remaining a top performer is the priority a company and its leaders place on these constituencies. They must be addressed in the order I have named them – customers first, employees second, and owners third.

A company's leader often must juggle many balls at the same time. However, there is usually one area of concern that primarily occupies the leader's mind – that subject that he or she thinks about when he or she goes to bed at night and gets up in the morning; that area where he or she has the greatest sense of urgency. In our studies, we have found that this area is usually one of the following four:

Solving each day's problems;

Beating the competition;

Profits (enhancing owner or shareholder value); or

Meeting the customer need.

Some leaders and managers spend their days reacting to and solving the problems that come across their desks. They go home at night feeling they have done a good job if their desks are clear at the end of the day. Not only are these leaders and managers not taking their companies anywhere, they are failing to recognize and understand that too much "firefighting" is a symptom of a company that is in bad shape – a company that does not have its elements in alignment and is not focused on its Mission.

Many leaders and managers are focused – even obsessed – with beating the competition. I agree that knowing what your competitors are doing is important, because they may have detected a change in a customer need that you haven't yet recognized. However, if your primary focus is on the competition, then you aren't focusing on the customer, and you will never be first – never in the lead. You will forever be reacting to someone else's moves.

Other leaders and managers focus on profits or enhancing shareholder value. In fact, most business schools still teach profits as the primary purpose of business. The CEOs of companies that are highly and consistently successful know (or have learned) that profit is a measure of performance – not the purpose or central focus of the company. If you send a message throughout the company that profit is the number one concern, then employees will make decisions and set priorities every day that are keyed and focused on maximizing profit rather than serving the customer. As we will discuss later, financial strength is important and, therefore, making a healthy profit is also important. However, it cannot and must not be the primary focus.

The *only* proper primary focus is the customer and his/her need. It is the *only* focus that can propel the company into a top performing position. All companies who are consistently top performers place the customer first in their list of constituencies.

Successful companies identify and select their customers.

Some companies try to be all things to all people. Successful companies know that by focusing on a selected customer segment, they can better understand and serve the needs of that customer, building a strong relationship and loyalty with the customer. Companies who serve the needs of their customer most closely will capture the hearts and minds of those customers. In turn, the customers develop a certain loyalty to that company and continue to do business with that company for reasons that go beyond price.

Companies who try to be all things to all people are trying to serve such diverse needs that they never develop a capability and reputation for serving any particular need particularly well. Therefore, because there is no other outstanding reason for a customer to decide to buy that company's products or services, price becomes the driving factor in the customer's decision to choose that company or another company. <u>All top performers have developed reasons other than merely price for their customers to continue to return to them for their needs that are served by that company.</u>

Successful companies differentiate how they serve the recognized need of the selected and identified customer in ways that provide real, recognizable value to the customer.

Differentiation is an important key to sustainable success. If a company understands that its primary focus is to serve the customer need and it clearly selects the customer that it chooses to serve, then it can develop ways to serve that customer's need that are clearly different from the other competitors who also try to serve that need. Moreover, successful companies differentiate themselves in ways that have clear and obvious value to that customer.

Dell Computer selected the business computer user and differentiated itself by selling directly to their customers with computers assembled to order and delivered quickly. Dell's computers are certainly not the cheapest. Nevertheless, Dell understood and met the needs of its selected customers.

After Steve Jobs was invited out of Apple, the company drifted, trying to enhance shareholder value. Jobs returned and brought back a fierce focus on the selected customer. Whereas those who led the company during the time he was gone tried to make Apple more like Compaq

Computer, Jobs re-instituted a distinct differentiation. The results speak for themselves.

When I ask companies how they are different, the answer I hear most often is that they are smarter. (I assume they mean that they are smarter than their competitors). I won't comment on whether or not they really are smarter, because it doesn't matter. The customer doesn't care whether or not you are smarter. The customer cares only about how well you are serving their need.

Highly successful companies differentiate themselves and maintain that difference. Unsuccessful companies don't differentiate.

Successful companies develop and promulgate prioritized values that truly reflect the business values of the leader and tell the employees how the company will operate on a day-to-day basis.

Leaders of successful companies know that the success of the company depends on the performance of its employees. Therefore, it is imperative that each and every employee understands the company's priorities, how the company wants them to conduct their day-to-day business, and what values the company holds as important. By developing, prioritizing, and disseminating its values, the company is giving its employees a simple, handy guide for their day-to-day actions. Without such guidance, employees will make it up as they go along or superimpose their own values.

All of the decisions, initiatives, directions, investments, plans, procedures, policies, actions, and reactions of the company are brought into alignment with the central focus and the Mission.

It is useless for the leaders and top managers to develop a clear understanding and plan for where they want to take the company if the rest of the employees don't know about it or have barriers and obstacles placed in their paths which hinder them from following the plan and achieving its goals. Most unsuccessful companies who think they have a plan have day-to-day procedures, policies, decisions, initiatives, incentives, directives, budgets, and investments that motivate and lead people to make decisions, take actions, and produce results *that are not in line with the plan.*

Leaders of successful companies ensure that every communication with the employee – every written document, every directive from a manager or supervisor, every training course, every incentive plan, every list of departmental and personal objectives, every behavior which is rewarded or discouraged – is consistent with the company's goals, objectives, plans and strategies. Everywhere the employee turns; everything he/she reads or hears; every decision he/she sees made by management; that employee sees consistency with the plan.

The leadership preaches the Mission throughout the company with a religious-like zeal and commitment. All employees buy into the Mission. And the buy-in takes place from the top down – in that order. (Those who don't or can't buy-in to the Mission must leave the Company).

Too often, we have seen top executives hold an all-too-infrequent meeting with employees and talk about financial measures, such as gross margins, profits, and inventory turns. This is a <u>major mistake</u> for several reasons:

Employees don't understand and don't care about such matters, because they generally don't understand the financial dynamics of the business and, to the extent that they do understand, they don't believe that, individually, they can affect these results (and they are right).

It turns the employees "off" to the prospect of employee meetings.

It squanders a valuable chance to talk about the customer, that customer's need, and the Mission - things the employee can relate to.

Leaders of successful companies have a deep sense of who the company is, where it is going, and how it is going to get there. They constantly communicate this message to the troops at every opportunity. Leaders of successful companies are forever talking about the customer and his/her need. They preach this to everyone in the company at every opportunity as if it is a religious conviction.

Every employee, including the CEO, subordinates his or her needs to the needs of the company.

High employee morale is important to a company's success. The morale at Apple, which was in the dumpster before Jobs returned, has soared. However, while the needs of the employees are important and are not ignored by successful companies, the needs of the business take precedence. The needs of the business must come first. Then and only then will the primary need of the employee - to be a part of a stable organization that controls its own destiny - be met.

Strategic Alignment

After I understood that successful companies have these Seven Guiding Principles in common, I asked what business management system I could develop that would help client companies consistently follow and adhere to these Seven Guiding Principles on a daily basis. In answering that question, I developed a powerful, new management system called Strategic Alignment, which, when installed and followed, provides a simple road map for adhering to the Seven Principles, thereby improving performance and exhibiting a new, high level of business excellence.

In a way, Strategic Alignment is not new nor does it depart from recent advances and thinking in management theory and practice. Rather it combines various advances in the art of management into a holistic view *that transforms the art into a science*, which can be studied, learned, and utilized by *anyone*.

Marketing experts have exhorted us to "delight the customer" with no clear explanation as to why this is important. In fact, many executives went through the following mental process.

"If I please the customer more than my competitor does, my costs will be higher than my competitor's costs. Yet if I can't charge more, my profits will be less. Therefore, what I should do is attempt to match my competitor in customer satisfaction."

We have heard this (or words to that effect) often. However, Strategic Alignment teaches us that you can and should charge the customer more if you delight him or her, *and the customer will be happy to pay it!*

The biggest tragedy has occurred in lay-offs, a practice that is so common and visible that it has fostered a whole new set of euphemisms – downsizing, "right" sizing, reorganizing. In England, employees who are laid off are referred to as "being made redundant".

During the Harold Geneen years at ITT, conducting a lay-off (this was prior to coining the phrase "downsizing") was a rite of passage from lower management into middle management. It was the way an ITT manager "made his bones". Never mind that, within three months, most of the employees who had been laid off were rehired or replaced with other employees at the same or higher pay rates. The lay-offs were widely heralded within the ranks of ITT's upper management, while the rehires went unnoticed.

Wall Street analysts and, in particular, fund managers love downsizing and will reward management with a temporary bump up in the stock price. If a downsizing is done as part of bringing the company into alignment, it is still tragic but is nevertheless necessary to save the remainder of the company. If, however, it is done to appease analysts and fund managers or because the CEO doesn't want to be the only one in his golf foursome who hasn't downsized, it has devastating effects on the company (including on those employees who remain employed at the company – the "survivors") with no offsetting benefits whatever.

Why do some companies succeed and others decline?

Success

Costco

FedEx

Apple

UPS

Starbucks

GE

Google

Decline

Western Union

AT&T

Sears

Toys R Us

K Mart

(These lists are representative of a few companies in each category and are not intended to be exhaustive.)

I also looked at companies that have succeeded and companies that have declined and asked, "Why?" For example, some of the companies shown above are continually successful and among the tops in their industries, whereas the other companies were once at the top but then declined. Are the executives at successful companies smarter? Did the others suddenly get dumb, or did the Board of Directors replace smart executives with dumb executives? I think not.

We all know of companies, such as Toys R Us, where the founding executive left and the company's performance declined. Was the founding executive a better or smarter manager? Again, I think not. There is another explanation.

Necessity is not only the mother of invention; it can also be the mother of strategy. Founding executives are often focused on the customer because they have no choice. This customer focus became ingrained, and the founding executive continued this customer focus because that's who brought him or her to the dance. Intense focus on the customer need is a central tenet of Strategic Alignment.

Sometimes, when the founding executive finally departs the scene, the replacement CEO is not as focused on the customer. When this happens, the company begins to drift into non-alignment, and performance declines. We have seen founders at Dell and Starbucks return to their companies to bring them back into alignment and put them back on the path to success. We have also seen other companies, such as UPS and Costco, where they made a successful transition from the founder to new leaders without missing a beat.

Strategic Alignment pulls all of these efforts, such as process re-engineering, technology improvements, technology upgrades, initiatives to "delight" the customer, and even downsizing, together into a whole. With Strategic Alignment, we understand the importance of these various initiatives. We also understand how and why they must all be in balance - aligned, if you will. If these and other elements are not aligned, each of these efforts, taken alone, will cost more and produce less (in some cases, a lot less) than originally hoped or promised.

In this book, I examine many companies' results, including some of the companies listed earlier. None of the companies we will discuss has been our client. My comments and analyses are based on public information, and my observations are "from the outside looking in".

All companies have problems. As we will discuss later, perfect alignment is an unattainable goal. Companies are constantly either moving towards or away from alignment. Therefore, there are always opportunities for improvement.

Also, most of a company's problems are usually not apparent to outside observers. When a company does appear to an outsider to have troubles, it's usually a safe bet that their problems are deeper and more severe than we can see. So, in most cases, the "troubled" companies I will discuss in this book are "more troubled" than we describe.

How can a business leader know if his or her businesses are out of alignment? There are several symptoms that are relatively easy to detect and which always indicate an alignment problem.

Low Margins

Companies who are not aligned have lower margins than their best competitors – in particular, lower gross margins.

Gross margin (or gross profit, if you prefer) is the margin that remains after direct costs are subtracted from net sales. Direct costs are those costs that in the short term rise and fall with sales; i.e. costs that are directly variable to sales volume.

For example, if a manufacturer's sales rise, the manufacturer hires more assembly line workers and purchases more parts (raw material, assemblies, components, etc.) that are needed to make the products. Conversely, if sales decline, fewer parts are ordered, and fewer workers are needed.

Gross margin dollars are available to cover indirect costs (sales and marketing, R&D, and G&A expenses). After we subtract these indirect expenses, we have operating margin, which becomes available to pay bank interest, taxes, and profit.

Within a narrow range, most companies pay the same in a given geographic region for workers. Also, within a narrow range, most companies should pay about the same for their material (assuming comparable quality). If these costs were all similar, then why would one company have a significantly higher gross margin percentage than another? There are two common reasons.

One variable might be price. There is a natural price range within which customers will pay for a product or service. If a company attempts to charge a price that is higher than the top of the natural price range, the customer will find an alternative for the product or service or do without, because the value of the product or service to the customer is less than the price asked. If the natural price range for the product or service is too low for a company to make a profit, then the product or service will be offered by the gray or black market (flea markets, etc.).

The company with the higher gross margin charges more for its product or service; e.g. at the high end of the natural price range. And why can they do this? Because the customer is willing to pay more. And why is the customer willing to pay more? *Because the value perceived by the customer, based on the total experience of doing business with that company, is high enough to warrant that price!*

The other driver of higher margins is that aligned companies have less waste. Strategic Alignment exposes wasteful investments and expenditures that are eliminated as part of the natural alignment process.

If gross margins are higher, then all other margins, including profit, can be higher. *Alignment is more important to margins than any other single factor, including size.*

Fighting Fires

As we will discuss later under Systems, the work performed in a business has three "system" elements: people, processes and tools (technology). The tools can be as simple as a hammer or as complex as a computer. The processes are the flow of tasks and activities.

- The quality of the process determines the effectiveness of the system;

- The quality of the technology determines the efficiency of the system; and

- The quality of the people determines the responsiveness of the system.

In an aligned company, systems are geared to satisfying a customer's need in an effective, efficient and responsive manner. Responsiveness is measured first by the ability to detect and recognize the subtle, ongoing changes in the customer's need; and secondly by the ability to act quickly and proactively on those changes.

In the mis-aligned company, responsiveness means fighting crisis fires. When firefighting becomes the accepted norm, it sets the standard for how we measure managers, which tends to be based on their crisis management skills. While the short-term perspective of crisis management appears to be responsive, productive and justifiable, from the long-term perspective crisis management is none of these things. In actuality, firefighting results from the need to "react" and "recover" from an organizational mis-alignment between the needs and wants of the customer and what the organization is actually delivering to that customer.

Many common symptoms of organizational misalignment, such as internal conflicts, customer complaints, and high employee turnover, are viewed or rationalized by some managers as events which lie outside the control of management. Therefore, the ability to fight crisis fires becomes a standard and desired quality of successful managers. As a result, the short-term goals of success, such as increasing revenues and cutting costs, receive the bulk of management's attention; and the direct connection between their daily crisis fires and the decay of business processes goes completely undetected.

Most managers do understand that responsiveness is very important, to the point that they have elevated responsiveness to the highest priority in the system -- above effectiveness and above efficiency -- and that, too, is a problem. *An organizational crisis is a result of an ineffective process – a misalignment between what the customer wants and needs and what the organization delivers.* The harder we work to respond to the crisis, the faster the process decays. As a process decays, the system needs more and more responsive energy to function. Then, we fill the short-term gap of a broken process with more people, because in the short-term perspective, people are cheaper.

We end up with more people and less process. Due to burnout and turnover, we are finally forced to change the people in the equation. Any remaining processes that exist begin to evolve around the skills and experience of the new people filling the short-term gap. With the loss of the more experienced people, additional people are needed the help fill a new gap. At some point, the "responsive people cost" is so high that we are finally able to justify the cost of bringing in additional technology.

So, instead of finding the proper balance of effectiveness, efficiency and responsiveness in our system, we end up with bureaucracy. Lots of technology, lots of people, weak processes, and customers who remain dissatisfied.

Most organizations tend to respond directly or indirectly to crises as a team. When they do, they stray from the mission as a team. The leader is also a follower, following signs and trends and carefully reading trends as "indicators," which can be internal as well as external. If there is a slight trend to drift away from the mission, perhaps in response to a crisis, and the trend continues without correction, the business faces the danger of "mission creep". In other words, *crisis management becomes the mission.* The leadership must be disciplined enough to bring the organization back to the proper Mission. *The most important role of the leadership of an organization is to keep the organization focused on the Mission.*

The next important role is establishing balance and alignment. Symptoms such as low morale and crisis management are signs many leadership teams fail to notice. Unfortunately, they are signs of misalignment and imbalance. Both management and leadership require skills of balance. For managers, it is balancing organizational systems. For leaders, it is balancing discipline and innovation.

Organizations that perform with excellence know the needs of their customers and have missions, strategies, structures and systems which meet those needs and exceed expectations. These organizations are aligned with the needs of their customers and in tune with themselves. Because they consistently fulfill the needs of their customers, crises and the necessity to respond to them are rare.

Internal Conflicts

An atmosphere of labor/management conflict indicates an alignment problem. Conflict among managers is also a misalignment indicator. Conflicts occur when there is disagreement on what should be done, how it should be done, or in what order things should be done. When there is no agreement on these issues, there is no direction. If there is no direction, there is no Mission. If there is no Mission, there can be no progress.

Customer Complaints

An aligned organization has relatively few customer complaints. One core ingredient of alignment is intense focus on the customer and his/her need. In aligned companies, an increasing trend in customer complaints is a key danger signal that the company is becoming less aligned and must take immediate action to reverse the trend.

Different Agendas

Whether the agendas are hidden or out in the open, if different executives and/or managers are marching to different drummers, the company is, by definition, out of alignment, because there is no commonly embraced

Mission. If there is no commonly embraced Mission, there is no Mission, irrespective of what the leadership might believe and profess. Different agendas are also a central cause of conflict among managers.

Employee Morale

Morale is directly proportional to alignment. The better the alignment – the higher the morale. The opposite is also true.

As they do with customer complaints, aligned companies track employee morale. If morale is improving, the company is moving towards alignment. If morale is deteriorating, the company is becoming less aligned, and it must detect and correct the causes.

Internal Focus

Companies that focus internally rather than on the customer need are by definition out of alignment. The most common internal focus is cost control or cost cutting. However, if you have no Mission and no Strategy, how on earth can you know which costs you can cut and which costs are necessary?

"They" versus "We"

A company's relative alignment can be gauged by a simple test. Have an outsider engage an employee in conversation. If the employee refers to the company as "they" rather than "we", the company is out of alignment. Moreover, the higher in the company the employee is who says "they", the more mis-aligned the company is.

Strategic Alignment begins and ends with the customer. Sandwiched between the customer's need and the customer's reward for choosing the company for his/her product or service needs are all of the focus, planning, actions and fulfillment engaged in by the company to serve the customer need. We refer to these elements - focus, planning, actions and fulfillment - as Directives, since they form a progression of activities and decisions throughout the planning and execution process that direct the company and its employees toward serving the customer need.

The next chapter will explain the Seven Guiding Principles and the corresponding Directives – one-by-one. Then, we will put them all together and discuss how and why Strategic Alignment is the one and only winning planning and management system for businesses that want to succeed, prosper, and endure.

Strategic Alignment Directives

Principle #1

The Purpose of a Company is to serve a recognized Customer Need. The Need must be recognized, not created.

VisiCalc – Recognized need

Computer Output Microfilm – Misunderstood need

Apple's Newton – Misunderstood need

Dow Jones Online Market Report – Misunderstood need

Strategic Alignment begins and ends with the customer and his/her need. *This customer need cannot be created in the mind of the company or its executives - it must be recognized and understood.*

This is the number one reason why start-ups which are funded fail. More than 40% of funded start-ups fail because when the start-up brought their product or service to market, there was little or no demand for it. The customer need was in the minds of those who started the company; it was not a recognized need that existed in the marketplace.

Fans of the TV show Kung Fu will say that the company's leaders must become "one" with the customer. The leaders must understand the customer need as fully and deeply as possible. If they can achieve this level of understanding, then they will "know" where that need is heading and will recognize and respond to changes in the need as soon as they are detected.

Above, we listed four examples of understood and misunderstood need. We'll briefly discuss each one in order to illustrate what we mean by recognizing, as opposed to creating, a need.

VisiCalc, written by a team of programmers under the direction of Dan Bricklin, was the first spreadsheet program. VisiCalc fulfilled at least two needs in the marketplace.

A spreadsheet was a godsend for managers who had to develop budgets, sales projections, etc. VisiCalc allowed them to do "what if" exercises without the need for a box of number 2 pencils and many erasers. You could change one number and instantly see the effect of that change on the bottom line without manually recalculating all the numbers. Prior to spreadsheets, developing a budget or a business model was a time consuming and error-ridden process.

VisiCalc also provided justification for those people (primarily engineers) who wanted their company to purchase a microcomputer for them. At last, there was now an honest-to-goodness, business-oriented program they could run on the machine, which gave them the justification they needed for the purchase.

Parenthetically, VisiCalc also produced two other effects. It just so happens that it was written for the Apple computer. (This was before IBM had entered the PC business. There were no clones, no standard M/S DOS operating system, and no standard Intel chip). Apple was merely one of many manufacturers of microcomputers. Today, all of the other microcomputer manufacturers of that time except Apple are gone, and while Steve Jobs deserves a lot of credit for what he did with the company, Apple should thank Dan Bricklin for writing VisiCalc for the Apple.

The other effect was that a young programmer on Dan Bricklin's VisiCalc team named Mitch Kapor later started a company called Lotus and developed Lotus 1-2-3, the first user-friendly spreadsheet program.

Therefore, although VisiCalc was a first of its kind, a new spreadsheet program when there were no such animals around before it, it was not a pursuit of a new technology for the sake of technology. It clearly fulfilled a need among customers - a need that Dan Bricklin recognized - and was very successful.

Computer Output Microfilm (COM) was not so fortunate. In the early 1970's, computer memory was still rather costly. Large users needed a method to archive old computer records and files without creating a mountain of paper (or so Kodak thought), and self-proclaimed visionaries were predicting that the "paperless" office was just around the corner.

So, a new technology - COM, which allowed the computer to write directly to microfilm - was developed. The industry - especially Kodak - loved COM. The trade magazines loved COM. The customers didn't need COM. While COM was being developed, the cost of memory began dropping like a rock. In the end, users merely added more memory to keep files active for a longer period of time, archived what they needed to keep on paper, and deleted the rest. COM was a dismal failure.

In the late 1980's and early 1990's, many within the PC industry thought that the handheld computer was the next big product. Apple spent a lot of R&D energy and dollars on the Newton – Apple's first Personal Digital Assistant (PDA). The product bombed and began a deterioration at Apple that continued until Steve Jobs returned to become Interim CEO. Some blamed the hand writing recognition software, which was not up to snuff.

Others blamed the lack of applications. The reasons don't matter. Newton and its other handheld computer brethren did not fill any recognized need.

Dow Jones, the Publisher of The Wall Street Journal, has been searching for two decades for new ways - primarily ways based on electronics and/or telecommunications - to package and sell the vast amount of financial news it gathers every day. During the mid-1980's they developed a service whereby they would broadcast over their own nationwide radio network news flashes about various companies. Subscribers would pre-designate which companies they were interested in hearing about. Based on the subscriber's input, Dow Jones would program and deliver to them a small box. Then, prior to each new announcement broadcast, the announcer would key into a keyboard a number unique to the company that the next news item was about. This unique number would be broadcast digitally prior to the news announcement. Your box would see the code and, if it matched one of your companies of interest, the box would turn on, allowing you to hear the announcement.

Dow Jones spent a lot on this service and launched it. It failed miserably. There was no need.

The first Directive in Strategic Alignment is the company's Purpose - a simple, one or two sentence statement of the recognized customer need and how the company will fill that need. Despite what many executives and business school professors might say, *it is not the primary purpose of a company to make money or "enhance shareholder value".*

There is an interesting phenomenon in business. Companies who focus on making money and enhancing shareholder value don't accomplish either - at least not very well. However, companies who focus on serving the needs of the customer make attractive returns, produce net cash, and maximize shareholder value.

Don't misunderstand. Financial strength is vital if a company is to survive, thrive, and grow. Financial strength is important for several reasons:

If a company has financial strength and positive cash flow (at least from operations), it controls its own destiny. If it doesn't produce net cash, others control its destiny.

Financial strength allows a company to remain independent, if it chooses to do so.

Financial strength provides leverage for acquisitions.

Financial strength provides flexibility to react quickly to changing customer needs.

Financial strength allows founders, investors, and key employees to reap the rewards of their risk and efforts without ceding control to others.

However, making a profit (or enhancing shareholder value) is the result of doing business and a measure of how well the company is performing - it is not the Purpose of doing business.

The Purpose of the company is - and must be - to fulfill the needs of the customer.

If you think this is splitting hairs and not all that important, take a look at Steelcase. This company dominated the modular office furniture market, an industry that took off when office cubicles became popular. Although many competitors offered similar systems at considerably lower prices, Steelcase continued to lead the industry in virtually every category. This was when the company was privately held. Then, the company went public, and the wheels came off.

From the outside looking in, it appears that their Purpose changed. After their IPO, they seem to have believed that their Purpose was now to "enhance shareholder value". As we will discuss in more depth later on, the signals that top management sends throughout the company establish the company's agenda and priorities in the minds of the employees. If the employees on the front line believe that profits have now surpassed serving the customer in priority, they will adjust their actions and decisions accordingly. This can lead to disaster.

Another company who made a similar mistake was Boeing. However, unlike Steelcase, Boeing's previous priorities were also flawed. We will discuss Boeing later, since prior to the current leadership, this company was a classic example of non-alignment.

Secondly, *the Purpose must not be to pursue a technology*. Technology is only viable and valuable to the extent that it fulfills some need of a customer. Technology for its own sake will not win.

Tacan, a company headquartered in Carlsbad, California, was involved in fiber optic technology for over ten years. Yet, the company never focused on any specific customer need. As a result, they languished while others in fiber optics soared.

It is also not the Purpose of the company to beat the competition. Beating the competition – like profits and higher market capitalization – is the result of adhering to the Seven Guiding Principles by implementing Strategic Alignment, thereby raising the bar of performance in your company. If you serve your customer better, know better where that customer's need is going, and get there first, *you will become the competitor to beat.* You will be the leader. Those trying to beat the competition will forever be followers, waiting to see where and how the competition moves and then reacting and responding to those moves.

Think of Purpose in the following way. What is the central theme of management discussions? What is the central focus? What does the leader go to bed and wake up thinking about? What issue creates a persistent sense of urgency in the leaders, managers and employees?

In order to follow the First Principle, central focus and sense of urgency must *always* be on the customer and his/her need. Other issues, while important, are secondary.

Principle #2

The Mission must Identify the Customer

As you might expect, the company's Mission, which is the second Directive, is the central tenet of Strategic Alignment. Three of the Seven Principles deal with the Mission.

The Mission is the guts of Strategic Alignment. This is not the mission statement you see framed and hanging in the lobby of many companies – a mission that says, in essence, "We will be the best at what we do, and our employees are our most important asset". In Strategic Alignment, the Mission Statement is a well thought out, hard-hitting, 1 ½ to 2 page statement of:

Who the customer is;

What that customer expects from the company;

What specific product(s) or service(s) the company will deliver to the customer;

How the product(s) or service(s) will be delivered; and

How the company will be *different* from the other companies who offer to serve that customer.

In its Mission Statement, *the company chooses its customers by selecting that segment of the overall market that it elects to serve.* By understanding the needs of the customers within that segment as closely as possible and serving those needs as completely as possible, the company will deliver maximum value and fulfillment to the customer, fulfilling the customer's expectations as closely as possible, and the company will receive maximum rewards; i.e. higher margins and loyalty from the customer.

Nordstrom, Target, and Costco have the same purpose, but their Missions are very different. They each target the specific needs of a specific customer whom they have identified and know very well. The same shopper may shop at Nordstrom in the morning, stop at Target around noon, and then head for Costco. However, that shopper goes to each store for very different reasons and with very different expectations. And in each case, those expectations are fulfilled.

Dell, HP, and Gateway have the same purpose, but Dell has a very different Mission. Dell built computers to order and sold direct – bypassing traditional retail distribution channels, and a single-minded focus on this Mission made Dell one of the largest and most profitable suppliers of computers in the world.

Principle #3

The Mission must Differentiate how the company will serve the Customer Need in ways that have real value to the Customer.

The Mission Statement is the heart of Strategic Alignment, and Differentiation is the heart of the Mission Statement.

Differentiation is vital. In the final analysis, there are two – and only two – strategies from which a company can choose if it wants to thrive, grow, and control its destiny. It can choose to be *the* low cost competitor in its geographic market(s), or it can clearly differentiate itself from its competitors. If a company does neither and attempts to be "all things to all people", it will find itself, like K-Mart, caught in the middle.

Top performing companies clearly differentiate themselves in ways that are important to the customer. Customers have very clear expectations when they do business with these winners and those expectations are consistently fulfilled. By intensely focusing on the need of specific customers, these companies, such as Target, Nordstrom, and FedEx, are, in effect, choosing their customers.

If you don't choose your customers, then your customers will choose you with needs that are diverse enough to keep you from maximizing value or clearly differentiating yourself from your competitors. This is often the main area where young companies falter. In a short-term effort to increase sales, they accept orders for products or services that depart from the product or service they intended to provide.

Appian Graphics was a young company that designed and manufactured video accelerator cards for personal computers. These printed circuit cards and accompanying software extended a single Windows desktop onto two or more video displays at the same time, allowing a user to, for example, have a Word document on one screen and an Excel spreadsheet on another with the ability to cut-and-paste from one to the other by simply moving the mouse. This is a powerful feature with many apparent and compelling uses. Appian Graphics agreed to a contract with a Japanese flat panel TV manufacturer to use Appian Graphics' core technology to produce a video card for the new "thin" TV. The Japanese company paid for the R&D

to adapt the technology for their particular need. The contract produced sales for Appian Graphics. However, the Japanese TV manufacturer owned the rights to the TV technology (since they paid for it). Much technical and management talent was drained to fulfill this contract; yet it did not fulfill the Mission and did not move Appian Graphics towards its Vision. Appian Graphics should have politely declined the opportunity. Instead, Appian Graphics was eventually acquired.

If you don't differentiate, your only other option is to become the low cost producer. There can be only one low cost producer (low cost – not low price!) in any geographic market and maintaining that position can be difficult. Just ask K-Mart or Woolworth, both of whom did fine until Wal-Mart, Sam's Club, and Costco came along. Toys R Us, a traditional low cost producer, failed to detect a change in the customer need - a change toward increasing demand for customer service.

Principle #4

The Mission must contain prioritized Values that truly reflect the business Values of the Company's Leadership.

The Mission defines who the customer is, what the company will do for that customer, and how the company will do those things differently than its competitors. The Mission also defines and prioritizes the company's values and principles. Values and principles are important to a company and its employees. Values and principles tell the employees what is important to the company, how the company will conduct itself on a day-to-day basis, and how the company expects its employees to conduct themselves.

The values should be well thought out and must reflect the true view of the company's executive management towards the business, the customer, the employees, the owners, and the community. The true test of values comes when the decision to stick with them is tough. If they are ever violated, it would have been better for the company to never have issued them in the first place.

Companies should always include the following four concepts in their statement of values:

- We will not make commitments to our customers, our employees, and our owners that we cannot keep, and we will keep the commitments we make.

- We value, respect, and trust our customers, employees, and owners, and we will strive every day to earn and deserve their respect and trust.

- We treat our customers, our owners, and each other honestly and truthfully.

- We obey the law.

Most employees develop very keen BS detectors early in their working careers. Everything executives do and say - how they spend their time, what decisions they make, what makes them frown and what makes them smile - must be in line with and consistent with the Mission and its stated values – 100% of the time. Once trust is lost, it takes a long time to rebuild it.

The values must also be prioritized. Many apparent conflicts exist in business. Quality vs. profit. Pleasing the customer vs. profit. Believing the customer vs. believing the employee. Values should be prioritized, and a "higher" value should never be violated in fulfillment of a "lower" value.

One of the keys to Strategic Alignment is the constant preaching of the Mission and values to all employees at every opportunity. Once they understand and embrace the Mission, the prioritized values, the Customer and his or her Need, the employees will then (and only then) have the knowledge they need to make day-to-day decisions that are in tune with the Mission without the necessity of checking with a manager. This is true empowerment and is an essential ingredient of the company's success.

Principle #5

All Directives of the Company must be brought in line with the Purpose and the Mission

In Strategic Alignment, we have segmented the functions or activities of a company into 7 Directives – Purpose, Mission, Vision, Strategy, Structure, Systems, and Performance. To facilitate discussion and understanding, we have listed these Directives separately. As we will discuss later, they are, in fact, intermingled and interdependent.

In top performing companies, these Directives are consistent with and in alignment with each other. We have already discussed the first two Directives - Purpose and Mission.

After the Mission comes the Vision - what the company will do in the future for the customer. Vision can be tricky. When a company is small, it should be a "one trick pony" - find one specific customer need, understand that need as much as possible, and fill that need as closely as possible.

Compaq Computer (which has since been acquired by HP) began by making the first, durable portable PC. (Actually, their first product is better described as "luggable" rather than portable). Soon, they got better at it and thrived. Later, as the company matured, it broadened its product line.

Ciena makes devices called Dense Wavelength Division Multiplexers (DWDMs). These products allow a telecommunications company to send many different signals over a single fiber optic circuit. DWDMs fulfilled a very real need for companies such as MCI Worldcom and Sprint, as telecommunications traffic, fueled by fax machines, cell phones, and ultimately, the Internet, grew much faster than had been projected. Ciena grew very rapidly and was courted by Tellabs for acquisition at a very attractive price.

Unfortunately, Ciena had failed to broaden its product line and its customer base. Essentially, the company had only one product - DWDMs. Moreover, the bulk of its sales came from two customers - MCI Worldcom and Sprint. When a possible sale of DWDMs to AT&T fell through at literally the last second, the merger also fell through. After reaching a price of $96 per share prior to the aborted merger, Ciena's stock price plunged into the teens.

Vision must include the broadening of products, customer base, and geography. Wanting to do these things is easy. Knowing when to do them is the tricky part.

Before it was acquired by HP, Compaq had moved way beyond the portable computer to providing a full range of computers and related products, such as servers. Dell has also expanded its product portfolio. Once the customer has developed a loyalty based on continuous positive experiences of doing business with a company, they are willing (and often eager) to buy other related products or services from that company.

However, while expanding horizontally, vertically, and/or geographically, a company must be especially careful not to jeopardize its alignment and those things that got it to where it is. This is why acquisitions can be so tricky and, too often, don't work. Many times, an acquisition prospect has alignment problems, which is why it is available at anything approaching a reasonable price in the first place. If an unaligned company is acquired, it is essential that it be brought into alignment ASAP, before it infects its aligned parent.

After the Mission/Vision comes the Strategy, a detailed plan of how the company will execute the Mission and make the Vision happen. The Strategy defines who will do what, by when, and with what resources to realize the Mission/Vision.

Before Jack Welch took the helm at General Electric, the company was languishing. Its sales grew annually about the same percentage as the GNP. Profits were "okay". Many analysts believed that the company was so big that it couldn't grow much faster than it did.

Welch had a different plan and a different Mission. In order to fulfill the Mission, he decreed that GE would not participate in any businesses in which it did not have (or couldn't attain) the number one or two market share. In order to realize this Mission, GE exited many of the businesses it was in. Because it is a very large company, GE also tended to focus on businesses where size matters, leveraging the company's size and financial muscle. Sales and profits began a healthy growth.

When many companies develop their "business plan", they begin with Strategy. In doing so, they sometimes commit two fundamental errors.

They assume that the path they are on is the right path, and

They assume that their competitors' positions and strategies will remain static.

Strategic Alignment teaches leaders to question everything often. Why are we doing what we are doing? Is this what the customer wants? Or needs? Should we be doing it at all? If yes, is there a better way?

One important output of the Strategy is the company's operating budget. In fact, a company's budget is a statement of its Strategy in financial terms – what it plans (and hopes) to accomplish in the future in pursuing its Mission and Vision. A company's financial statements – primarily its income statements – are a statement in financial terms of how well (or poorly) it actually implemented its Strategy in the past and how well the Strategy was aligned with the Mission in the first place.

Taken together, the Mission, Vision and Strategy constitute the Leadership Directives and are the responsibility of the company's leadership - primarily the CEO. (The subtitle of this book is *The Playbook for the CEO*). By carefully developing a comprehensive, customer- and company-specific Mission and preaching that Mission at every opportunity throughout the company, the leadership of the company is freed from day-to-day micro-management and is now able to monitor and refine the Mission, so that the company and the Mission remain in tune with the ever changing need of the customer.

Next comes the Structure, which defines – usually in writing – how the company is organized and how it operates. Structure includes (but is not limited to) the business financial model, the business plan, the budget, employee manuals or handbooks, organizational charts, compensation plans, training manuals, training curricula, quality programs, policies and procedures.

A few years ago, Boeing had many problems. (Obviously, if you achieve a 60% share of a large global market and you lose millions in the process, it goes without saying that you have problems). If you turn back to the beginning of this book and review the symptoms of non-alignment, those symptoms described Boeing a few years ago.

For several years, Boeing's Mission was to increase its market share. There are subtle but important differences between Boeing's Mission and GE's Mission. Besides the fact that this Mission does not respond to a Customer Need (the customer couldn't care less what your market share is), the rest of Boeing's Directives were not in alignment with the Mission. One of the elements of Structure is the financial business model a company uses to guide decision making and the day-to-day management of the company. Boeing's financial model assumed that the company would become more efficient as volume increased. This led the company to lower the price of its aircraft.

In the past, Boeing had manufactured superior planes and had received premium prices. As a result, Boeing essentially owned the market among those airlines that wanted, and could afford to pay for, top of the line aircraft. This was Boeing's customer and its differentiation. If Boeing had defined its market as the market for top quality aircraft, it could have, rightfully, declared victory.

However, Boeing didn't do that. The company decided to be all things to all people. In order to sell more planes, it had to sell to companies that either couldn't, or wouldn't, pay the premium price based on the value inherent in Boeing's planes. In other words, they were attempting to sell their planes to customers who did not necessarily want the value that had been recognized and sought by Boeing's traditional customers.

Imagine that Nordstrom decides to increase its market share by going after J C Penney's customers. While maintaining its high level of service and product quality, Nordstrom slashes prices, drawing in Penney's customers but losing its shirt in the process.

As implausible as that might sound, it's exactly what Boeing did. The company cut prices without cutting costs.

Their financial model and other parts of the company's Structure and Systems were not in alignment with the Mission. The more planes the company assembled and sold, the more money it lost.

Boeing then changed its Mission to "enhancing shareholder value". In doing so, they replaced one bad Mission with another bad Mission.

Boeing has since righted the ship. Moving the corporate headquarters from Seattle to Chicago was an important ingredient in their current success, because it made it easier for management to focus on the customer rather than the unions.

The financial model and the budget must accurately reflect the dynamics of operating the business in line with the Mission and in pursuit of the Vision. Both must in essence be a financial statement of the Strategy, since budgets contain the dimensions of time and resources.

In Strategic Alignment, *there is a clear distinction between frugality and cheapness.* The frugal company does not waste. Strategic Alignment clearly exposes those activities within the company which are not in alignment with the Mission. Once identified, these activities are eliminated, removing waste and creating true savings.

The cheap company, on the other hand, attempts not to pay full value for those resources it needs to fulfill its Mission. This in itself is anti-alignment and, while possibly producing short-term savings, serves as a large obstacle in the path of fulfilling the Mission.

Companies who have downsized for the wrong reasons have discovered that this type of savings is illusory at best and, in fact, can cripple the company in its efforts to thrive and grow by serving the customer need. *Budgets which are derived from and are in alignment with Strategic financial models and dynamics cannot be "trimmed" without creating a negative effect on the Mission.*

Likewise, all the other elements of Structure must be in line with the Mission. The structure of the organization itself – the org chart - should be driven by the customer need and the optimal structure to fulfill that need. Companies sometimes organize around personalities. However, no one person transcends the Mission. The employees must adapt to the Mission. You cannot adapt the Mission to the employee, because the Mission focuses on the customer and the customer does not care about the individuals in the company. The Customer cares only about how responsive the company is to his or her need.

The Structure of the company is the skeleton of the organism. It provides the framework within which employees fulfill the need of the customer. Every element of the company, particularly the Structure, must be continuously examined to uncover the obstacles that lie between the employee and the fulfillment of the Mission. Once detected, the obstacles must be rooted out.

All of the elements of Structure must be in tune with the Mission. If not, Structure – not Mission – will define and guide the employees' day-to-day actions and decisions.

After Structure, we have Systems – the people, technology, and processes that, together, produce the products or define and deliver the services. This is where the "rubber meets the road" and where most of the time, energy, and money of the company are invested.

In a manufacturing company, the Systems include the assembly workers and all of the technology and processes that procure and bring in the parts, distribute them to the floor, track the products through the manufacturing cycle, inspect the finished products, transfer the products to inventory, and eventually ship the products to the customer.

It also includes all of the tools, test equipment, machinery, and other technology used by the workers to manufacture and test the products as well as to track and control the flow of material on the manufacturing floor.

The Systems must be in tune with the manufacturing strategy, which itself must support the Mission. A company can design to order, make to order, make to forecast, or make to inventory. Which manufacturing strategy the company selects must be in response to the customer's need and the company's Mission, and all other Directives must be in alignment with this manufacturing strategy.

In a service business, such as fast food, the actual restaurants themselves are the Systems – the employees who take the order and prepare and serve the food along with the processes and technology they use to take and record the order, control inventories, ensure quality, and prepare and deliver the food as ordered.

Wendy's implemented a strategy of cooking and preparing their hamburgers to order, rather than cooking them in advance and keeping them warm until sold. Wendy's had identified an unfilled need. When Wendy's entered the market, there were three large players – McDonald's, Burger King, and Burger Chef. The prevailing wisdom at the time said that there wasn't room for another nationwide hamburger fast food company. Wendy's made room by fulfilling an identified, unmet need and displaced Burger Chef, who faded and disappeared.

Regardless of the actions of executives and managers, the customer need is either met or not met by the Systems. If the employees do not know about, understand, and embrace the Mission, there is no hope of maximizing the customer's reward by meeting his/her need and expectations as closely as possible.

Process re-engineering and technology upgrades take place at the Systems level. As you can now see, if the processes and technology are not aligned with the higher directives of Mission, Vision, Strategy, and Structure, then all of the improvements and upgrades in the world won't help. They will still be the wrong processes and technology. Only now, the investment in them will be higher.

Systems also must be horizontally aligned - aligned among themselves. The people, processes, and technology must be balanced. During the 1990's, too many companies concentrated on advancements in technology – both manufacturing and computer technology – without commensurate advancements in processes or increased training for the people who use the technology. The weakest link analogy works here. Systems will be no better and no more effective than its weakest component.

After Systems, we have Performance, the output of the Systems. Performance is the product or service that is delivered to and perceived by the customer. This is the face of the company that the Customer sees – its products/services, the people who answer the phone at order input or customer service, the sales people, the brochures and other printed material, the investor relations communications. These day-to-day, minute-by-minute encounters with various company employees establish the perception of the company in the mind of the customer. If they are all aligned one to another and all are focused on meeting the need of the customer that the company has selected to serve, the perception of the customer will be very positive and the customer will return time and time again, *regardless (within a broad range) of the price.*

The Structure and Systems constitute the Management Directives and are the responsibility of Management. In a sense, the *Leadership is concerned that the company is doing the right things*, while the *Management is concerned that the company is doing those things right.* By aligning the Structure and the Systems with the Mission/Vision and Strategies, Management ensures that it is removing the obstacles that stand in the way of the employees following and fulfilling the Mission and delivering precisely what the customer needs.

When all of these elements are in close alignment, the company focuses its time and energy on meeting the needs of the customer and avoids wasteful uses of resources that are not in line with the Mission. Also, by effectively communicating the Mission throughout the company, Leadership gives the employees the information they need – empowers them, if you will – to make the day-to-day decisions that are in tune with the Mission without having to rely on Management to make every decision. This frees Leadership to focus on the Mission and lead, and it frees Management to focus on the Structure and Systems, insuring that they remain aligned with the Mission.

The Aligned Business

In the aligned business, Leadership Directives create Values and priorities that guide managers and employees in day-to-day decisions, allowing Managers to remove obstacles between the Mission and the employees, so that employees can meet or exceed the customer's expectations, such that the customer's highest expectations are realized and the company is rewarded with loyalty and high margins.

In the aligned company, Leadership and Management have different responsibilities.

Leadership recognizes and understands the customer need. This is a never ending task. While it is understanding the customer need better and better, the leadership nurtures the Mission to fulfill that need in a way that differentiates the company in the eyes of the customer, and ensures that the Strategy makes the Mission happen. Leadership focuses religiously on the Mission and preaches it constantly to all employees.

Management ensures that the Structure and Systems are balanced among themselves and in alignment with all higher Directives, especially the Mission. Management also identifies and removes the obstacles that stand in the way of the employees fulfilling the Mission and meeting the customer need as closely as possible.

All of the Directives align with and support the Mission. Any activity that does not support the Mission is eliminated. There is a clear distinction between cheapness and frugality.

Everything begins and ends with the customer. The customer has a need. If the business aligns itself to meet that need as closely as possible, the customer's expectations will be met as closely as possible. The entire experience the customer has of doing business with that company will be positive. Therefore, the value the customer perceives will be high, and the customer will be willing to pay a premium to do business with the company. The company has now given the customer a reason other than price to buy from it, a necessary ingredient in achieving a sustainable competitive advantage.

Strategic Alignment is holistic. In order to describe and explain this system, we have presented the Directives individually and depicted them in a two-dimensional hierarchy. This is similar to studying the human body. You study anatomy, separately from the central nervous system. Then, you may learn about the gastric system. You may study the heart and blood distribution system along with the lungs and the respiratory system, or you may learn about them separately.

Similarly, we have isolated the various Directives within a company in order to study and understand the dynamics of each. We have also presented them as existing separately in a hierarchy that begins with the Customer Need and ends with Performance and the Customer Reward.

All of the Directives are in fact intertwined and interrelated in a three dimensional sphere that is surrounded by the customer. Every element flows into and derives output from every other element. Information, knowledge, and understanding must flow seamlessly and without interruption throughout the company, from the CEO to the production line worker. Everything that happens – all decisions, all communications, all activities, all spending – must be in alignment and harmony with the Mission and the Vision.

Perfect alignment is unattainable. The Company is either moving towards or away from alignment.

Customer needs change.

An aligned company will grow. It can't help but grow. Growth means additional employees who don't yet know or embrace the Mission. Growth means new processes and new technology.

Tough decisions must be made. If the Values are compromised, alignment slips.

Conflicts can arise between the discipline required to adhere to the Mission and the creativity of many employees. Creativity is vital to the company in detecting and adjusting to changes in Customer Need. The challenge of leaders and managers is to channel creativity into areas that are aligned with the Mission and Vision.

Ensuring that the Mission remains aligned with the current customer need, that the Vision is in tune with where the customer need is headed, and that the other Directives remained aligned with the Mission are never-ending tasks.

The Non-Aligned Business

In a non-aligned business, the Company chases profits rather than Customer Need. The Opportunity is "created" in the Company's mind rather than recognized. There are hidden agendas, unclear direction and miscommunication. Customer Needs are not fully understood. Strategy cannot "see" Need and tries to align with Mission, but is hampered by poor research & inaccurate data. Structure attempts to accommodate all higher Directives, and because these higher Directives are not in alignment, creates 'high overhead" and bureaucracy. This non-alignment results in tight cash and earnings, which restrict investments in technology and people. To make matters worse, some of what is spent is wasted. The result is that the Customer reward is not optimized and the Customer goes elsewhere.

As you can see, if the Directives are not aligned, the focus is lost, resources are squandered, and, worst of all, the needs of the customer are only partially met, resulting in low margins, tight cash, missed projections, employee frustration, and poor performance.

Different companies are driven by different forces. They may be:

Earnings Driven

Manufacturing Driven

Asset Driven

Expense Driven

Inventory Driven

Owner Driven

Strategic companies who align the elements of the organization are <u>Customer Driven</u>, and these are the companies who continually rank at the top of their industry.

The Keys to Success

There are several keys which are vital in managing for success through the implementation and practice of Strategic Alignment.

Customer Need

Leadership must be in tune with the customer and his/her need. There is an important difference between customers and markets.

Markets don't exist; customers do. Markets are merely a convenient way to amalgamate groups of customers who make independent buying decisions for a variety of reasons. Moreover, the groupings can be defined in such a way to tell any story you want to tell. In Strategic Alignment, the target market represents those customers who will place the highest value on the company's differentiation. In developing its business model and strategy, it is obviously important that the target market be large enough to support the company's growth and provide the financial support to achieve its goals and fuel future growth and profitability. A target market that is too small will not sustain the company. Conversely, a target market that is too large may not respond favorably to the company's differentiation.

Markets don't buy anything; Customers do. Individual customers make independent buying decisions. We cannot understand and respond to the needs of a market, because a market doesn't have needs. Only customers have needs that the successful company will recognize and fulfill.

Customer needs change in real time. Market trends reveal *after the fact* that the customer needs began to change at some point in time in the past.

The Leadership must get past market numbers and get to know the customer and his need. This usually means spending sufficient time "in the field" "touching" the customer; finding out what "floats his or her boat". This task cannot be delegated to the sales force. The job of the sales force is to sell the products or services that the company currently provides. The responsibility of the Leadership is to insure that those products or services – today's and tomorrow's - remain aligned with the customer need.

Not only does the customer need change; sometimes that change can be sudden and significant. Earlier, we discussed the natural gross margin range of a product or service. In this concept, customers will pay more or less for a product or service within a certain range based on how well that product or service fulfills their need and expectation; e.g. how much value they place on the product or service and the total experience of doing business with the company providing the product or service.

However, that margin range can move. For example, years ago, we saw a sudden, significant lowering in the margin range of personal computers. This change was caused by a collective realization that computer hardware was largely the same in performance and reliability, regardless of which company provided it. The mystique had been removed, and personal computers became more of a commodity. A margin range continues to exist; the top end of the margin range has simply moved downward.

Companies who failed to detect this trend early enough were caught with bloated inventories and no new lower cost products. By the time they detected the movement by watching the market trend, it was too late. Those companies, such as Dell, who kept in touch with the customer, detected the trend as it was happening.

Principle #6

The Leader must preach the Mission throughout the Company with a religious-like zeal and commitment.

The roles of leaders and managers in the company are distinctly different. One of the many key aspects of Strategic Alignment is that by defining and communicating the Mission and values throughout the company and thereby empowering the Managers and employees to make day-to-day decisions aligned with the Mission, Leadership is freed from micro-management and is now able to lead.

The Late Admiral Grace Hopper was in her time the highest-ranking woman in the Navy. She is also credited with developing a leading computer programming language – COBOL. More important to us, she understood the difference between management and leadership. She said the following:

"You cannot manage a man into combat, you must lead him. You manage things, you lead people."

"While excellent management requires the most extensive understanding of processes to be managed, excellent leadership requires the most extensive understanding of people to be led."

"Managers try to do things right. Leaders try to do the right things."

Leadership's job is to keep the organization focused on accomplishing the Mission, while ensuring that the Mission is the right Mission. Management's job is to eliminate the barriers to accomplishing the Mission, implementing the

Strategies, and providing the Structure for the workers to responsively accomplish the Mission, using processes designed to optimize effectiveness and technology fitted to optimize efficiency. While Leadership is responsible for the development of the Mission and the Strategy, Management is responsible for the development of the Structure and the Systems necessary to implement the Mission and the Strategy.

Some believe that leaders are born, not made. On the other hand, there is a thriving industry devoted to Leadership Training.

There are several skills or personality profiling systems available to help gauge an individual's aptitude towards effective leadership. Our favorite is the MBTI.

The Myers-Briggs Type Indicator (MBTI), a personality topography based on the work of Carl Jung, defines 16 different personality types. Within these personality types, some are predisposed towards becoming leaders and others are not. This fact has several implications for companies.

First, using MTBI (or a similar methodology) to better understand and know the managers within an organization would be one important factor in determining who should be placed on a track to rise to positions of formal leadership. Perhaps more importantly, an organization's structure should allow "natural" leaders to surface. Given half a chance, they <u>will</u> surface. Denied that chance, they will usually leave the company. On the other hand, whether or not a person's MBTI predisposes him or her towards leadership, anyone will become a better leader with leadership training than without it.

As the guardian of the company's values, *it is vital that the Leader's actions be in synch with the company's values 100% of the time*. The effectiveness of Leaders is dependent on their ability to recognize the distant horizon

(Vision), determine the point of convergence (Purpose and Mission), chart the course (Strategy) and communicate to the followers. By communicating the company's directives in a simple, clear, and consistent manner, the objective is never in doubt. Each and every employee is then empowered to succeed by acting on behalf of the customer within the boundaries of the Mission and the prioritized values and, therefore, requires little or no supervision.

With the training and empowerment of the employees, Management is free to "eliminate the barriers" that prevent those employees from delivering on the Mission. These barriers may include non-aligned Structure, Processes or Technology, skill enhancement, resources, mentoring, coaching, and conflict resolution.

Communications

Having determined the Customer Need and developed the Mission which states how the company will fulfill that Need in ways that are different, thereby increasing the value to the customer of doing business with the company, Leadership must communicate the Mission throughout the company.

The Mission must take on religious aspects, and the Leader must communicate the Mission with an intensity approaching religious fervor. One of the keys to Strategic Alignment is the constant preaching of the Mission and values to all employees at every opportunity. Once they understand and embrace the Mission, the prioritized values, and the Customer Need, the employees will then (and only then) have the knowledge they need to make day-to-day decisions that are in tune with the Mission without the necessity of checking with a manager. This is true empowerment and is an essential ingredient of the company's success.

I want to repeat something I said earlier. I have seen top executives hold an all-too-infrequent meeting with all employees and talk about financial measures, such as margins, profits, and inventory turns. This is a major mistake for three reasons:

Employees don't understand and don't care about such matters, because they generally don't understand the financial dynamics of the business, and, to the extent that they do understand, they don't feel that, individually, they can affect these results (and they are right).

These types of meetings turn the employees "off" to the prospect of employee meetings.

These types of meetings squander a valuable chance to talk about the customer and the Mission, things the employee can relate to.

Leaders must have a deep sense of who the company is, where it is going, and how it is going to get there. They must then constantly communicate this message to the troops at every opportunity. If Leaders do this without let-up, the company has a real chance to win.

Principle #7

Every employee, including the CEO, must subordinate his/her Needs to the Needs of the Company

Early on, at the time of start-up and for a while thereafter, the company does not have an existence in and of itself. True, it is a group of people (or maybe just one) who have joined together for a common purpose. But during this period, the company can die quickly (over a weekend), if, for example, key people depart.

At some point, though, the company takes on a life of its own. It becomes a separate, "living" entity. The people can leave; the location can change; even the products and/or services it provides can change. But the company survives. If death does come, it comes slowly.

It is often difficult to know when this "birth" occurs. However, we do know that it occurs, at the latest, when the company reaches sustained operational positive cash flow or when the company takes on significant debt (whichever comes first).

Why is this concept important? Because after the company is "born", it is imperative that every employee – from the CEO on down – subordinate his or her needs to the needs of the business. *Without this subordination of needs by all employees, differing agendas will arise and mis-alignment will inevitably follow.*

Where does the competition fit into all this? In case you haven't noticed, we haven't stressed competitors very much. Sure, it's important to know and understand what the competition is doing and where they are heading. However, too many executives become fixated on the competition. It becomes their central focus, and they spend too much time and energy responding to the competition.

If you are forever responding to the competition, you are letting them define the game. They are the ones breaking new ground and finding new ways to meet the customer need, and you are always following; always behind; always late.

If you align your company with a truly differentiated Mission focused on fulfilling the customer need, you set the pace. You become the competitor to emulate. You are out front. You become the one to beat.

Implementation and Measuring

Let's restate the 7 Guiding Principles in Strategic Alignment terminology. The 7 Guiding Principles believed in and adhered to by companies who attain and sustain a position at the top of their industry and consistently exhibit exceptional performance and produce exceptional results are:

The Purpose of a Company is to serve a recognized Customer Need

Profit is a measure of the Company's performance, not its Purpose

Beating the competition is the result of alignment

The Purpose must be based on customer need, not technology

The customer need must be real, not in the mind of the company

The Mission must identify the customer

The company must address customers who will recognize and reward the company's differentiation

Attempting to be "all things to all people" will dilute the differentiation to the point that the value is eliminated and price alone becomes the determining factor

The Mission must differentiate how it will serve the customer need in ways that have real value to the customer

The Mission must contain prioritized values that truly reflect the business values of the leader.

The values must be followed without exception

No higher value can be compromised in pursuit of a lower value

All Directives of the company must be brought in line with the Purpose and the Mission

The Leader must preach the Mission throughout the company with a religious-like zeal and commitment.

All employees must buy into the Mission.

Understanding and acceptance of the Mission must be obtained from the top down – in that order.

Every employee, including the CEO, must subordinate his/her needs to the needs of the company

Balanced Scorecard

Perfect Alignment is an unattainable goal, which leadership must constantly strive to approach. All organizations are continually moving towards, or away from, alignment.

After the theory, methodology and tools of Strategic Alignment have been put in place, the company should establish four sets of metrics, referred to as a "balanced scorecard", in order to monitor its progress and detect trends towards non-alignment as soon as possible, so that early, corrective action can be taken.

Most companies rely on financial results to guide their performance and to institute corrective actions. While financial results are the first element of the balanced scorecard, they are, in fact, the most lagging indicators in the scorecard. It sometimes takes a few months for waste, once identified and "eliminated", to wash its way through the company's financial statements. Also, trends have inertia. Alignment improvements must first slow and then reverse negative trends. Relying solely on past financial results is like steering a boat by watching its wake.

Many companies also track quality, which is the second element of the balanced scorecard. Quality measures are also lagging indicators, but they do reflect more recent trends than are indicated in financial statements.

In many companies, "quality" means the MTBF (mean time between failures) of a product. In Strategic Alignment, quality means everything that the Company does that "touches" the Customer – the product or service itself, the total responsiveness of the customer service personnel to customer inquiries (not merely answering the phone within 3 rings), the customer friendliness of the invoice and the responsiveness of the accounting department to billing inquiries, the helpfulness and truthfulness of sales personnel, etc., etc., etc.

Quality must be quantified and measured constantly. If quality trends begin to slow (or turn negative), the Company is already moving away from alignment

The third part of the balanced scorecard includes customer complaints and attitudes. While many companies pay attention to complaints, few have a structured, systematic way of tracking customer attitudes and their trends on a consistent, ongoing basis. Customer attitudes are a current indicator. A consistent, objective method for quantifying and tracking customer attitudes must be developed and implemented. This is a touchy process, because simply asking customers too often about their attitude towards the company and its products or services can irritate the customer and create negative attitudes – the very thing the process is attempting to avoid. If the customer attitude index is slowing or turning negative, the company is in the process of moving away from alignment.

The fourth element of the balanced scorecard, and *the only leading indicator*, is employee morale. The positive morale of a group is a powerful energy source. If morale is good, it can energize the entire organization and manifest itself in positive customer interaction. If morale is low, it can, like a cancer, suck the energy out of the strongest members of the organization. In very close competitive struggles among equals, positive morale is often the deciding factor between success and failure.

As we discussed earlier, most of the resources within a company are expended at the Systems level, which consists of people, processes, and technology. The components of the Systems come together to support, produce, and deliver the company's products or services to the customer.

While the quality of the processes determines the effectiveness of the systems and the quality of the technology determines its efficiency, *the people determine the responsiveness* of the systems. Employees with high morale and positive attitudes are more responsive than those with low morale and negative attitudes. If employee morale is improving, you are moving towards better alignment, and if employee morale is deteriorating, you are headed for misalignment.

Employee morale will normally elude the impersonal nature of surveys and extends beyond the grasp of simple statistics. And yet it is the best indicator of the company's alignment and whether the company is moving towards or away from alignment. Since morale is vital to the organization's future well-being, how does the company measure it and, then, having measured it, how does the company improve it?

In our experience, morale can only be measured through one-on-one interviews. Employees' morale is a direct reflection of their sense of worth and respect and their optimism for their near-term future. Confidence and integrity feed this. Confidence reflects the employees' belief in their own competence, and integrity reflects their trust in the organization.

Therefore, by elevating competence and trust, the organization elevates confidence and integrity, which elevates optimism, and that, in turn, elevates morale.

Because only 5% of the employees who take an anonymous survey believe that it is truly anonymous, surveys are, at best, unreliable and, at worst, misleading. Carefully orchestrated one-on-one interviews, where an environment of political neutrality and social contribution can be established, will produce information with greater depth and applicability than will surveys.

Once we have measured morale, how do we improve it? First, leadership must understand and accept that everyone in the organization is important to the success of the organization and, therefore, deserves equal respect and trust.

The leaders are not better, nor more important, than the managers. The managers are not better, nor more important, than the workers. All have different jobs requiring different levels of skill, capabilities, knowledge, and experience. Leadership's job is to keep the company focused on accomplishing the Mission, ensuring that the Mission is the right Mission. Management's job is to eliminate the barriers to accomplishing the Mission, implementing the Strategies, and providing the Structure. The worker's job is to "responsively" fulfill the Mission, using processes designed to optimize effectiveness and technology fitted to optimize efficiency.

In order to do this, the worker must be treated fairly and with respect, and he/she must know, understand, and embrace the Mission and Strategies of the organization. Armed with the prioritized values that arise from consistent, aligned Missions and Strategies, they then can be empowered to do their jobs.

Employees in such an organization will have high morale and positive attitudes, and they will be highly responsive to the Mission and to the needs of the customer.

There are very good consulting firms who specialize in working with companies to develop and implement balanced scorecards to meet that company's specific needs. However, this should not be used as eyewash. The balanced scorecard should be implemented only after the company has made substantial progress towards aligning itself and its Directives. Otherwise, the baseline that the company establishes in its metrics will be too low.

It is not sufficient to understand Strategic Alignment. If a company is to realize the full benefits of this powerful system, the leaders must embrace and believe in Strategic Alignment. If the Leaders fully accept and submit themselves and the company to Strategic Alignment, the company can attain and maintain sustainable competitive advantage over its competitors, because it will have a customer-centric, unique business model which, because it mirrors the beliefs, values, and personalities of the Leaders, cannot be duplicated.

Strategic Alignment frees Leaders to lead. The single most important responsibility of the CEO is to develop and promulgate the company's Mission. Communicating the Mission is a never-ending task. Every employee must understand and embrace the Mission with its values and priorities. Once this is understood throughout the company, *then (and only then)* can employees be empowered to make day-to-day decisions that will be in harmony with the Mission.

Strategic Alignment frees the leaders from day-to-day micro-management. It teaches the Managers that their primary function is to remove the obstacles that hinder the workers from performing efficiently and productively, and it shows the Managers how to do it. And by communicating the Mission, Strategy, and Values clearly and unambiguously to the workforce, Leaders and Managers empower the employees to fulfill the identified needs of the customer with high morale and a strong sense of worth and accomplishment, while reducing wasted efforts and wasted resources to a minimum.

Finally, Strategic Alignment is the gift that keeps on giving. The longer that Leaders and Managers use Strategic Alignment, the better they get at understanding the need of the customer and at honing the company's differentiation. The longer the customer experiences the rewards of doing business with the aligned company, the better they understand the company's Mission and their expectations become even more closely aligned with the company's performance. And the longer the employees hear the Leader talk to them about the customer need, the more they will understand the customer and the more they will trust that the Leaders and the Managers are walking their talk.

This is why the competitive advantage is sustainable. The aligned company keeps evolving and getting better and better. The competitor who tries to catch up by watching and emulating the aligned company can never catch up because they are attempting to emulate last year's model, while the aligned company has continued to grow and has become something else – an even better something else.

Aligned companies:

Are Strategic;

Know what they are and what they want to become;

Keep focused;

Place the customer first;

Trust their employees;

Continuously communicate with their employees; and

After the employees understand the Mission, the Customer, and his or her Need, Empower their employees to serve the customer need.

Companies who do these things outperform the companies who don't.

About the Author

Robert K (Bob) Bennett

After a career in the telecommunications industry serving in executive positions in sales, general management and mergers & acquisitions, Bob developed Strategic Alignment and started his consulting firm, working with clients in the Pacific Northwest to install this powerful business planning and management system in the clients' companies..

Bob lives in the USA near Seattle, Washington with his wife, his son (a college student), one dog, and one cat. He also has an adult son who lives on the East Coast and an adult daughter who lives in Seattle.

You can contact Bob at rkbennett@msn.com